Writing for Zero Position

TERESE KERRIGAN

Copyright © 2021 Terese Kerrigan

All rights reserved.

ISBN: 9798746418333

DEDICATION

I dedicate this book to my family, friends, mentors and anyone who pushed me to publish. Without your unconditional support and never questioning my "why," this information never would've made it out of my head and onto paper. For that, I am forever grateful for each and every one of you. You know who you are.

CONTENTS

	Acknowledgments	i
	Introduction	iii
I	What is SEO?	Pg 1
II	SEO Writing Hacks	Pg 11
III	Even More Content Ideas	Pg 33
	SEO Reputation Management Playbook	Pg 35
	Additional Resources	Pg 38
	Glossary of Terms	Pg 39
	References	Pg 41

ACKNOWLEDGMENTS

Thank you and good luck to everyone in the SEO community.

INTRODUCTION

Each of us, amateurs and professionals, needs to attract new audiences who choose to buy from us. I'm a digital marketing pro and I sold you this guide. Thank you for buying it. Use it to optimize your content. Use it as inspiration or for writing prompts. Use it to manage your online reputation. But above all, use it to crush your online competition, "push down" negative search results and alleviate writer's block.

"But my basic knowledge of SEO may be different from what you think is basic." You're in luck because I start this guide off with a breakdown of the tools I use, why I use them, and how I use them to create a future-proof strategy for search engine optimization. I will give you the dos and don'ts of SEO. Beyond the basics, I will give you my secrets to writing for search engines.

I cannot promise your website or blog will rank over your competition. No digital marketer can and anyone who says they can is lying to you. I can, however, promise to give you "Ah ha!" moments and writer's block breakthroughs. You will attract more likes and shares on social media and visits or clicks to your content. These visitors will be engaged and in-market, meaning their visit will most likely convert to a sale or whatever your conversion goal may be.

This guide will show you how to structure your content in a way that's desirable to search engines and your audience. It will explain the nuances of technical SEO. I included two bonus chapters with five new writing prompts and a SEO reputation management playbook that I only give to my clients. A glossary and appendix list terms and tools. You'll find all useful when reading this guide. I'm excited for you to write your best content ever and for it to be seen by your audience.

Everyone dreams of scoring the top position on Google search results. While that spot can never be guaranteed or permanently secured, you can learn how to write in a way that says to search engines, "Hey, look at this awesome content I just published that is helpful to thousands of monthly searches."

Just because top search rankings are not guaranteed, you should not be discouraged. I encourage you to leverage my experience and successes. Tweak your content and test it. Testing and measuring analytics are how to find out if your content is performing well or not.

Write often. Write every day if your schedule allows it. Feed your inner artist with exercises and creative writing prompts that I'm about to give to you. Content is king. Get your content seen with my tips for writing for zero position.

WHAT IS SEO?

When defined, search engine optimization seems like common sense. You ensure people who are searching for your keyword can find your content by using your keyword in the copy of your content. But it involves much more than that. Your rank in search results depends on a number of factors like keyword density and usage, website health and speed, backlinks and mentions as well as other off-page factors like a strong social media presence or authorship. I will define these terms like keyword density and backlinks in the glossary at the end of this book.

Dictionary.com defines search engine optimization as "the process of maximizing the number of visitors to a particular website by ensuring that the site appears high on the list of results returned by a search engine."[1]

MOZ defines it as "search engine optimization (SEO) is the practice of increasing the quantity and quality of traffic to your website through organic search engine results."[2]

What these definitions fail to explain is the nature of SEO. It's volatile, meaning it changes frequently. It's systematic, meaning there's a right and wrong way to proceed. Over the course of my professional career, I've used techniques that were once seen as best but are now seen as "Black Hat" or spammy. Ever since the first Google update in 2012 known as Panda, digital marketers have been penalized for playing dirty. It's important to know the difference between good and bad SEO so that you don't fall prey to the pretty promises offered by black hat SEO tricksters.

Yes, old techniques do fall to the wayside. You might then wonder if this guide is outdated by the time, you read it. Good news! There's no expiration date on the actionable writing I include, and you can use my tips to write blogs, ad copy, brochures, billboards, flyers, taglines and more. I've also included my brand essence questionnaire, which explores who your brand is and how it operates in the marketplace. Besides the basic SEO principles and tools, you'll find evergreen material you can use to sharpen your brand's authority.

Not everything new is good for you. Modern technologies present new technical SEO challenges (or opportunities) for websites that want to be found when users are searching for their product or service. Google dominates the search engine market with almost 1.2 trillion searches per year.[3] According to Google, 20 percent of searches in the app are by voice-to-text.[4] How do you optimize your site for voice-to-text searches?

If you follow Google's best practices for SEO now, your website will still be optimized for voice search. To leverage voice-to-text technology in your favor, start by auditing your content to ensure you use natural speech patterns. Keep reading this guide for more about natural speech and why it's recommended. While traditional SEO methods tell you to intelligently place keywords in the title, meta description, image filename, and throughout the copy, you will need to monitor and possibly change how you use text on your page.

How to Optimize Your Site

1. Keep up with best practices for SEO.

Google Search is the dominant way people find information online. To be ranked among top searches, your website needs to be fast and serve relevant content that's qualified by backlinks and brand mentions. Voice search doesn't change our need to search. Voice search changes how we express that need. Consider all the enhancements to location tracking that make local search more intuitive, which eliminates our need to qualify search keywords with a zip code or city name.

Laying a foundation is the first step to having good SEO, so why wouldn't that be true when optimizing your website? Maybe you were told that all you need is a logo and a blog to achieve a high ranking in search results? Whatever the case may be, you may not know all the factors involved in the Google Search algorithm.

There are two categorically different search engine optimization methods: On-page and off-page. Neither method is more important than the other. Both works together to give the appropriate signals to search bots. Search bots or "spiders" crawl the Internet, reading text and some code, to hunt for newly published or edited content. The algorithm chooses which pages will appear for search queries. You can't outsmart the algorithm. Trying to do so is known as black hat SEO. Black hat tactics like keyword stuffing and buying backlinks send the wrong signals to search bots. If your site appears to be "spammy" or trying to cheat the algorithm, your whole website can be de-indexed. Yes, Google and other search engines can decide whether to show your website at all.

I suggest using free tools that let you see what optimization signals you're sending to site crawlers.

Below are a few of my favorites:

Google Analytics

Google gives you free tools that work together to help you monitor and fix errors that may be keeping your site from ranking high in search results. Analytics connects with Google Search Console. Analytics gives you data about your site traffic and user behavior. Analytics lets you monitor on-page SEO metrics like bounce rate, time on page, and page load speeds.

Google PageSpeed Insights

This tool lets you know how fast your content and code loads. Page load speeds are incredibly important to your ranking. If your page takes too long to load, it may have a higher bounce rate or a low traffic. Those technical SEO factors can prevent your website from being seen on the first page of search results.

Google Search Console

Crucial on-page or technical SEO factors are monitored here. This tool will help you with Schema, sitemap indexing, page crawl issues, and mobile or desktop UX errors. Schema is a markup language that provides site crawlers with additional information that only they can read and consume. Schema is what is used to generate featured snippets. I go into depth on this topic later on, so continue reading.

Bing Webmaster Tools

This tool is Bing's equivalent to the Google Search Console and Google Analytics. While Google still dominates user search, you would be ignoring up to 25% of U.S. web traffic by not monitoring your Bing search data.

GTMetrix

GTmetrix is like the big sister to Google PageSpeed. Not only does it analyze technical SEO health, but it offers free advice on how to fix errors like minifying CSS or HTML, parsing Javascript, and image resizing.

Yoast SEO for WordPress

If you use WordPress as a content management system or CMS then you've likely heard about Yoast. Yoast provides a checklist that helps you score on-page SEO while you're writing a new page or post. Yoast SEO is a free plugin that helps you manage SEO page titles, meta descriptions, and your robots.txt file. The robots.txt file tells search bots what or what not to include when it crawls your website.

SEMRush

I use SEMrush for competitor analysis, keyword research, backlink audits, and for monthly site crawls. This function lets you see what search engine spiders or bots see when they scan your website. Keep in mind, you can only perform one site crawl per month with a free account. There are many tools like SEMRush, but I found that this one is the best free-to-use off-page technical SEO software. It helps you analyze competitive factors like keyword ranking and backlinks. Perfect for keyword research and backlink and featured snippets discovery, SEMRush is a not-so-secret weapon of mine.

I set up all these tools and more so that I can monitor your SEO health. Savvier clients like to sign into their accounts to double check my work or discover user insights on their own.

Google Penalties: What Not to Do

Knowing what users are searching for is the nexus between your site and traffic. Keyword research determines the best keywords to optimize your content for. However, going overboard can send the wrong signals to Google and Bing so pay attention to these key penalty types:

Over-optimization

As I mentioned above, Google doesn't like it when you stuff keywords. Keyword stuffing is considered black hat SEO, not good SEO. I discourage anyone from using black hat methods as a get-SEO-quick scheme. It fails as a long-term strategy. The Yoast SEO plugin helps you calculate keyword density, so you aren't at risk for over-optimizing a page. I strategically sprinkle keywords in body copy, headings, and metadata to avoid a penalty.

Long-tail keywords

Choose one focus keyword per page and make sure this keyword phrase is two to three words long. You can use other free tools by Google to discover long-tail keywords. By writing in a natural way, I can almost guarantee that your content is automatically optimized for long-tail keywords. In voice search, context is key. What you say and how you say it will be future SEO best practices. Get ahead of the curve by future-proofing your optimization techniques. I share my technique to develop a list of long-tail keywords in Section II.

Latent Semantic Indexing or LSI

LSI helps you find search terms used in natural language. While there is no evidence to support LSI's role in SEO, I believe there will be in the future. For example, synonyms and supporting words help define a keyword phrase that may have more than one meaning.[5] If your website helps people find pricing quotes on auto insurance, then search queries for "quotes from automakers" don't fit the bill, but queries for "cost of car insurance" do match. Tools like the LSIgraph can help you find keywords associated with your content.

Implement on-page SEO techniques to improve search rankings. I mentioned a few on-page SEO signals above, but here are the important ones that matter most:

URL Structure

Keep your URLs short and sweet. The URL or "Uniform Resource Locator" signals site structure to Google and the keywords in page titles or URLs can send positive or negative signals. The Yoast SEO plugin helps identify common issues with URL structure. Make sure your URL doesn't contain any stop words like articles of speech (the, a, an) and conjunctions (and, but, or).

Page Title

A good SEO tactic is putting your keyword closer to the beginning of the title. That can be difficult to achieve but it can make all the difference in your position on the search engine results page (SERP). The 70-character title should be short and relevant to your focus keyword.

Image Titles

Choose unique descriptions for your image file names before you upload them. This gives you another chance to insert your keyword if it is appropriate to do so.

Alt Tags

Tactfully use keywords in your image alt tags if the keyword helps describe the image. Not only can your content rank in search results, but it can also rank in image and video search results as well.

Meta Descriptions

This is the 155-word blurb that describes the page in search. This is a great place to put LSIs. You only have two lines to communicate how your page is different from the other pages in SERPs.

Headings

Insert keywords in h1, h2 and h3 tags to organize your content and spread out your keyword uses.

External links

Research content is better quality. Therefore, Google rewards you for linking to other websites. If you're worried about adding too many links, you can add a "nofollow" tag to the < a href > link to tell Google spiders that more information can be found off site. Having too many external links can make your site look like a link farm and Google will penalize you. I optimize by embedding at maximum three external links. The same way you want to link to external sites, these external sites want to link to you. This is called backlinking. Backlinks signal to the Google Search algorithm that the content is of high quality. Websites with a high Domain Authority, like news sites and .edu or .gov websites, carry more weight toward your backlinking score. Keep reading for tools on how to find your backlinks and those of your competitors, so that you can build a solid backlink profile.

Internal links

Google also wants to know how your content relates. Link to other pages on your site or blog to connect ideas and concepts. All of your pages should link to one another in order to create a path for the Google spider to crawl.

Site Structure

Your site should be easy to navigate. You can achieve this in a number of ways, but mainly by creating a searchable text box for your content. From the time the page loads, the user should not have to click multiple times to find what they need.

Why is keyword stuffing dangerous?

It's a black hat SEO technique. Black hat is a term that marketers use to describe a strategy that goes against best SEO practices. Search engine algorithms have learned to identify spammy websites that repeat the same keyword over and over. Sophisticated algorithms are designed to serve the user, providing the best answer to their search queries. As voice search builds momentum, websites will be battling for the coveted zero position.

How do you avoid stuffing your content with keywords?

There are a few obvious uses of keyword stuffing that everyone should avoid. It is still a best practice to use keywords in titles, tags, file names and meta descriptions, but you need to make sure the placement helps the user find what they're looking for.

Here are two examples of egregious keyword stuffing that you should not do if you want to boost your search rankings:

1. High Keyword Density

The number of times you use your keyword in the content is important, but there are different ways of optimizing for a keyword without obvious repetition. There is no cut and dry keyword density, but most marketers stick to a keyword density of 2% or less. Yoast encourages plugin users to aim for a keyword density between 0.5% and 2.5%. You can do a keyword density audit of your competitors too! If you're wondering what the density is for the top-ranking website, all you have to do is count the number of times the target keyword is mentioned on the landing page and divide that by the total word count.

2. Invisible Keywords

Believe it or not, SEO used to be as easy (or disingenuous) as to hide keywords in the background. Yes, marketers once camouflaged keywords by making the text the same color as the background. The same caution can be applied to using keywords in certain tags. Search bot spiders crawl text, html and some script, so it may seem advantageous to unnecessarily include keywords in your website's code or in image alt tags. Google Search Console allows you to add a separate image sitemap, which helps your images be found in Google image search. By jamming keywords into the alt tag or file name of an image, you may be adding to the clutter and not helping someone who is using contextual keywords to find a matching image.

2. Know how people are searching for your product or service.

We don't search the way we did five years ago. We're using longer sentences and natural speech. We speak or type our queries the way we talk to a friend. It's harder to target natural speech because we use different colloquialisms, syntax, languages, and articles of speech. Google has stopped listening to articles of speech like "the" and "a/an" because they don't add to the meaning of a keyword. Other articles of speech like adjectives combined with nouns create long-tail keywords.

I talk in depth on how to develop a list of long-tail keywords in Section II.

Enter competitors into SEMrush to analyze their keyword density, page rank, and backlink profile. That information helps you determine your benchmarks for gaining position in search results. Improve on what your competitors do to become first in search results.

Identify how people are finding your website, but don't stop at a list of keywords. You need to identify your brand essence - your unique brand positioning - in order to brainstorm a new list of natural language queries. To optimize for voice, create content using common speech patterns and long-tail keywords.

3. Adopt a Q&A-style content framework.

The best way to earn the highest organic position in search is to capture a featured snippet. A featured snippet is known as position zero because it sits above all other organic results and is highlighted by a thick black border. I help my clients develop featured snippets for their site because it's best to give people (and Google) what they want. And it's a long-term way to protect your organic marketing revenue. Do you have a frequently asked questions section on your site? Are you answering the questions your customers are asking? Structure your site using bulleted and numbered lists to leverage Google's featured snippets for additional site traffic.

4. Write with authority.

Google knows if the content author is a spammer or if they're a real authority on the topic. There are many things you can do to signal your authority to Google. Start by making your author's name transparent. Ensure your blogs or articles have an author name associated with them by marking it up using Schema for articles. Another way to show your authority is to link out to quality websites that backup your message. You can do this via linking to external websites and by embedding video and images on your website.

5. Speed things up.

Are you compressing images before you upload them to your site? Do you have too much JavaScript firing before your content, keeping your technical SEO score low? If your site doesn't load within 30 seconds, you might have a creeping bounce rate. Audit your site for large files and perform a website speed test to ensure the health of your on-page SEO.

Speed is vital to your website ranking. To calculate your website's speed, there are three tools I use:

Google PageSpeed Insights

In July 2018, Google released a speed update to force websites to become fast and secure for mobile users. This tool helps you learn about mobile resource requirements and to help you reduce web bloat.

SEMrush

If you're not sure how to fix errors you may find, ask your IT professional or web developer. You can also search online for quick fixes, which is how I find my solutions. Make sure you always backup your website (i.e., template files, post files, media, etc.) before you attempt to change server settings or your .htaccess file.

10 SEO WRITING HACKS

Frequent content creation may seem daunting. That's why I came up with this list to help you hit required word counts and hurdle writer's block. It took me more than a decade to discover these tips. I promise they make writing for SEO easy, fun, and lucrative.

1. Write for Zero Position

Google the target keyword and look for any auto-generated questions. Provide better answers to featured questions on your site.

If you sell widgets, your customers may be looking for widget sales. In the below example, "widget sales" is our target keyword. Perform a Google search for "widget sales" to see how featured snippets have changed since I finished writing. At the time of publication, our search query had returned a featured snippet and suggested similar search queries.

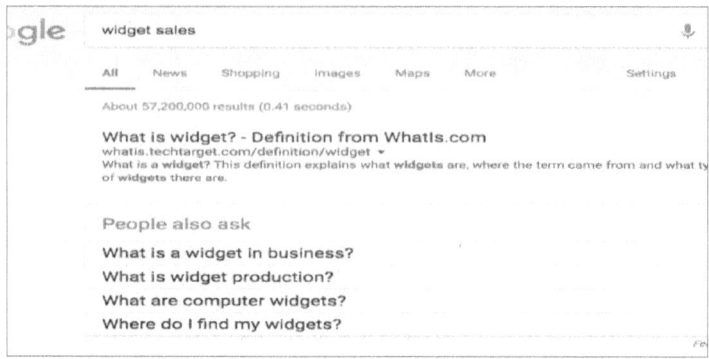

Screenshot taken of a Google Search for the keyword "widget sales"

The featured snippet contains a definition for widget. Notice, contextually, the snippet does not exactly match the query. Marketers refer to this match type as a broad or phrase match type. Match types are familiar to pay-per-click marketers because that's how we control the ads that appear for keyword variants. If you want to steal this featured snippet (assuming it has a high search volume), you can produce content that specifically answers any questions or topics related to widget sales.

Our search query also features a suggested search snippet that gives you similar questions asked about that keyword. You can earn zero position for these questions as well. Featured snippet boxes are a gold mine for digital marketers who want to expand their keyword mix to attract new audiences.

Don't know your target keywords? Head to #2 to learn how to develop a list of keywords that deliver the ultimate return on investment.

What is zero position?

Having zero position in SERPs means your page ranks above all other organic results, but still below the first two paid positions (if there are any). Featured snippets occupy the very first position in Google search results or SERPs. Earning a featured snippet is one of the fastest ways to get on the first page of Google. Examples of featured snippets are Google My Business listings, Wikipedia references, recipes, instructions, definitions, comparisons, pricing tables, "best of" lists, and frequently asked questions.

WRITING FOR ZERO POSITION

How you structure your content for zero position depends on the type of featured snippet you're targeting. For instance, if you want to rank for comparisons then you'll structure your data in HTML tables. Google will pull its best answer and depending on the query that answer can be in the form of a paragraph, numbered list, bulleted list, table, YouTube video, image or data chart.

4 Rapid Steps to Winning Zero Position

1. Sign up for Google My Business. You'll need to verify a physical address for your business.
2. Edit a Wikipedia page for your subject matter and add to the discussion with relevant information and source links back to your reference material.
3. Create a table and list your menu. Include prices, item descriptions, brand names and other relevant shopping information.
4. Use Schema to markup your images, videos, lists, address, URL, author information, and more. Visit Schema.org to learn how to embed structured data on your website. Structured data aids site crawlers by helping to parse and categorize your content. Marking up your data does not require much technical knowledge. All you need to know is basic HTML to mark up your data. If you use a content management system (CMS) like WordPress, there are many SEO plugins out there that can help you mark up your web pages.

Why is the first page position so important?

There are several benefits to winning a featured snippet and the coveted zero position. Traffic volumes will vary by website; however, generally speaking, featured snippets send more traffic to your website. Users who use ad block software will see your website first. And earning the very first organic spot gives your content credibility.

As talk-to-text voice search grows, you'll see more emphasis placed on featured snippets. When a user asks a voice assistant to answer a question, the voice assistant will find the single best answer available. Often times, that answer is the very first search result. The featured snippet can vary depending on word order and keywords. For this reason and others, featured snippets are more volatile than the first SERP position. Focus on supplementing long articles or blogs with concise, formatted lists or charts.

2. Keyword Variations

Google several variations of your target keyword with different endings or pluralization.

Let's dive more into match types. I believe they're more important to organic search than previously considered. In my experience, if it is required for paid search advertising than it is likely important to organic search too. Here are the basic match types that search engine algorithms use to deliver search query results. Match type rules vary by search engine, so please consult guidelines for each source (i.e., Google, Bing, Yahoo!, etc.).

Exact Match

An exact match occurs when a user's search query is identical to the target keyword. Exact match search query results have higher click through and conversion rates because they perfectly match.

Examples of an exact match:

Target Keyword:

widget sales

User Queries:

widget sales
~~how many widgets sold?~~
~~widget sales in 2017~~

Phrase Match

Phrase matches aren't identical or perfect matches. The majority of organic searches produce phrase or broad match results. Think about how often we misspell words, especially on our mobile device. Search engines don't want marketers to create content for misspelled words. Since phrase match results are not exact, they tend to convert at a lesser rate than exact match.

Examples of phrase match:

Target Keyword:

widget sales
widget sales in 2017

User Queries:

sales of widgets for WordPress
2010 plugin and widget sales
widget sales

Broad Match

You can think of the broad match type as a wildcard that helps you target search queries that may or may not yield a good answer. Broad match types help you capture queries where the user may use a synonym or similar word.

Examples of broad match:

Target Keyword:

widget sales
gadget sales

User Queries:

who sells widgets?
~~widget sales~~

The Golden Rule

The SEO rule is plain and simple: only use keywords when they help the user find what they're looking for. Moreover, offer content that is unique to your website. Others may copy you but consider it a form of flattery and an opportunity to freshen up your message. Target keywords that attract queries which generate a return on investment. Just because you rank for a keyword doesn't mean you will generate revenue. If you're starting your website from scratch, you may not have historical ROI data available to you. In those cases, you must analyze current SERPs and decide which keywords have the most projected ROI based on search volumes.

How to Develop List of Target Keywords

Develop a list of target keywords by analyzing competitor keywords and researching keyword search volumes. Use free tools like Google Analytics, Google AdWords, SEMrush, or Google Search Console to find long-tail search queries that should generate the most traffic to your site. Once you have a list of five keywords, plug those into Google Search to discover websites that currently rank for your target keywords. Meet your online competition.

4 Steps to Keyword Research

Step 1: Find historical search query volumes for your site traffic in Google Search Console or Google Analytics. Enhancements to Analytics like Ecommerce Tracking can be set up by your website administrator. By implementing a few lines of code, your Analytics dashboard can show you real-time ROI from online sources.

Step 2: Sign up for a free Google AdWords account to use their Keyword Planner tool. Find new keywords based on similar keyword groups and forecast search volumes to see which keywords are the most valuable.

Step 3: Perform a Google Search on each keyword to discover a list of websites that rank for that keyword, then plug these competitors into SEMrush.

Step 4: Use SEMrush to find gaps in your keyword list. You'll need your list of competitor websites from Step 3 to do this.

To future-proof your SEO, focus on context as much as content. If you want to associate your service with safety, then consider making those connections for the reader **and** the search engine. A single word can completely change the meaning of a target keyword.

Be sure to target long tail keywords that fit your objective. If your call to action is to purchase, you may want to focus on cost-related content instead of how-to content. If you want to build traffic and engagement, you may want to focus on shareable content like videos, whitepapers, and infographics.

Take these three very different queries, for example:

"How to fix a toaster"
"How do toasters work?"
"How much do toasters cost?"

While the target keyword "toaster" is the subject of each query, its meaning changes depending on the words that appear before and after the keyword. The user expects to find content that matches the context of their query.

Here are examples of content you may offer for each query:

"How To" content ideas:

Explainer videos
Instructional guides

Whitepapers or client case studies
Infographics
Checklists

"How Things Work" content ideas:

Explainer videos
Diagrams
Whitepapers

"How Much" content ideas:

Cost comparison charts
Customer testimonials and reviews

3. Repeat What Works

Read top ranking sites for content ideas and gently borrow - don't steal - from the best.

With your list of target keywords, you can begin to optimize existing pages, implement alt and title tags, and hunt for featured snippet opportunities. Don't miss opportunities by being afraid to repeat what works.

Here is a list of examples again for reading convenience.

Featured Snippet Examples:

Google My Business listings (e.g., Google Maps for local search)
Wikipedia references
Recipes
Articles
How-to instructions
Word definitions
Product comparison charts
Price comparison tables
"Best Of" lists
Frequently asked questions

You don't have to perform a Google search for every target keyword in order to determine if a featured snippet exists. If you're feeling lucky, use SEMrush's position tracking tool to find featured snippets for your target keywords. SEMrush will show you if a featured snippet exists for your target keyword and which site holds that position. It is easiest to win "best answer" for an existing featured snippet than it is to get Google to rank your help page or blog. Search engines have a single mission to provide answers to questions most often asked by their users, who are not necessarily your audience. Increasing traffic is great if that's your goal, but conversions are better. You must keep your eye on ROI if you're selling products or services online.

I don't recommend formatting every blog as a listicle or bulleted lists of questions with answers. I do recommend phrasing your headings as questions and writing your copy as answers. Rewrite long blocks of text as bulleted lists, but don't replace your content with nothing but lists. Create infographics, videos and other visual content that helps answer high volume search queries.

Keep your copy concise and brief. Content is king and you should include at least 750 to 1,000 words on your landing pages. Break up the content with your lists, images, videos, external links, charts, tables, and other featured snippet content.

4. Repurpose

Pick up to three blogs or articles on your site that address the target keyword topic. Write a summary and link to related content.

An old blog can become relevant again when you link to it from updated content. Repurpose your content. Don't cannibalize your content. Bring something new to the discussion and include a link to the previously published blog as part of your internal linking strategy.

There are numerous reasons why repurposing a blog benefits the reader. As the years go by, new ideas emerge from every industry and so do new audiences. By developing several blogs on the same topic, you can become the digital authority on the topic.

Reasons to Update a Blog:

Outdated facts and figures
New Author Perspective - New Point of View
Include Current News
Changes to Staff
Newly created videos or graphics
Changes to the Marketplace
Tailor to a New Audience or Persona
New Call to Action
Emergency Information/ weather updates

5. Reblog

Pick up to three external resources not on your site that address the target keyword. Write a summary and link to the related content.

Repurposing your content saves time, but it doesn't add value unless you refresh your target keywords, source materials, or visuals. You can use the same technique when linking to external sites. Have you ever seen a blog written elsewhere that was just amazing? You think, "Why didn't I think of that first?" You wouldn't be the first publisher - amateur or professional - to have that thought. The good news is, you can reblog that amazing article too.

The Tumblr app made reblogging a popular term. Reblogging refers to sharing content with your network and adding a comment or quote. It's also very similar to the concept of quoting a tweet or posting a few words along with a retweet from another Twitter user.

How to reblog

Congratulations, you found an article you want to reblog. It's well-written and cited and comes from a well-known publisher. Score.

Your next step is to develop an angle for your blog. Do you agree with the original author? Do you take an opposing stance on the topic? Write to a different audience or tweak your call to action. Taking a different angle on a topic can generate unlimited ideas for new blogs.

Break down the referenced article into a new outline and circle the points that are the most intriguing. Turn those points into a list. Maybe the original author wrote in paragraph form and you can reblog their original idea along with a graphic you created or a list. Use the writing for zero position tips you've learned to reconstruct an idea into something new and original. Never steal! Always give attribution to any quotes or graphics you use. Find new source materials and links that support your opposing opinion. Use recent data and dates to freshen up an article that may be out of date, but still newsworthy. By the end of reblogged content, you should have more than 750 words. Don't forget your basic optimization techniques and naturally place your target keywords in headings and metadata.

6. Upsell

Pick up to five related products or services that a user may find helpful and write about it.

Whether your goal is to sell products or attract website visitors, you're missing out on opportunities if you don't upsell. You don't necessarily have to upsell a product or service, either. You can upsell information too. Any time you link to additional content, you're technically upselling or giving that backlink authority.

Take an online blogger for example. What would she upsell? If she's writing a book review, she can upsell the book itself using a referral marketing link. Many online marketplaces, like Amazon, allow users to create unique referral links. When users click and buy from your unique link, you earn money. It's that easy.

E-commerce sites that don't upsell related products on single item pages or during checkout miss out on last minute add-ons. You could be leaving a significant amount of revenue on the table by not drawing connections between two or more of your products. If you sell tech products, then upsell batteries or expandable memory.

If you sell homeowners insurance products, then you might be affiliated with mortgage companies, brokers, title companies, home improvement stores, or inspectors. You may not be able to earn money from referrals to these sources, but you will be helping your readers which is your ultimate goal if you want top position in search results.

Here are more ideas for how to upsell information, products, or services.

If you sell information or your sole purpose is generating traffic to a blog, then you can upsell by:

Linking to related blogs
Referring related products (Amazon Affiliates)

If you sell goods, then you can upsell by:

Linking to related products that work together
Embedding customer reviews and feedback to related products
Linking to products that are often purchased together
Selling multiple items as a group

If you sell a service, then you can upsell by:

Embedding customer reviews and case studies about related services
Grouping services to sell as a package
Linking to blogs that build trust in combining services

Not only can you upsell by creating a need during the checkout process, but you can incorporate these ideas into your email marketing strategy as well. Send emails to customers regularly and upsell, upsell, upsell!

7. Show and Tell

Create a video and include a video summary and a transcription.

YouTube videos can earn zero position too! Google purchased YouTube in October 2006. Since then, YouTube videos have appeared in search results. Perform a Google search for "how to make a sandwich" to see where YouTube videos appear in SERPs.

If you're an avid YouTuber than you're in luck. By transcribing your videos, you can optimize the content of your video. As long as you cite your source, you can even write a blog that transcribes a video that belongs to another creator.

Steps to optimizing videos:

Use your target keyword in the video title
Use your target keyword in the video description
Tag your video with your target keyword
Write a transcription of the video
Publish the video and transcription in a blog on your site
Link to your blog from the video's description
Share your blog on social media for more likes and traffic

8. Survey Says

Survey your customers, review their feedback, and identify trends that can help you fill gaps in your content.

Do you leverage your customer reviews to build trust? If so, great! You can use your customer feedback as the basis for a case study blog. If you don't currently collect or monitor your online customer reviews, then keep reading. In this chapter, I break down the importance of reviews and suggest tools to help you manage customer feedback. But first, let's explore how we can leverage customer reviews to generate compelling content.

Online reviews are generally polarizing, meaning they're either really bad or really good but rarely in between. Collecting and listening to customer feedback is an important part of the buying cycle, especially if your business plan relies on repeat sales from a single customer acquisition. If I can offer one single piece of advice on this topic, I encourage you to reply to every review. Good or bad, your replies signal to future buyers that you listen and care. You have the power to control your online reputation although it may seem like it's out of your hands. Keep your replies neutral and sincere. Offer a discount or upgrade, if possible.

Writing and Optimization Ideas

Write a press release and blog about how you raised your customer satisfaction score from X to Y.

Call out a negative review and write a case study on how you used the feedback to improve an area of your business. Did you switch suppliers? Change your shipping company? Use a different type of packaging? Find the opportunity in your negative reviews.

Embed positive reviews on landing pages to boost consumer confidence. Some of the tools I mention below, like Trustpilot, offer integrations that let you place a snippet of code anywhere on your website. You can tag and group your reviews to control which reviews are enabled for view.

Share positive reviews on social media. Make fun graphics with your reviews to boost likes and engagement.

WRITING FOR ZERO POSITION

How Reviews Impact SEO

Online reviews signal authority and trust to search engines. To combat fake news, search engines use online customer reviews to determine a publisher's trustworthiness and rate their product or service. Perform a Google search for "Times Square" and look for the Trip Advisor result.[6] You can see users gave Times Square a high rating of 4.5 out of 5 stars.

Google Search screenshot showing star rating

Those stars are known as seller ratings. You can obtain seller ratings for products or services, and you can use free or paid methods to obtain them.

What are seller ratings and how do I get them?

Seller ratings appear in organic and paid search results. A star-rating indicates trust to users and to search engines. You can find your seller ratings across search engines like Google, Bing and Yahoo! Google leverages various review sites to collect and report your reviews as a number. This number gets displayed on a 5-star rating scale under your site's title in search results. On the contrary, Bing leverages Yelp reviews to report seller ratings in search results.

The Top 5 Third-Party Review Sites

1. eKomi - Unlike other costly review sites, eKomi offers a bit more brand control. Brands get a chance to not just collect, reply and publish reviews, but a chance to review customer feedback. And before that feedback posts publicly. Full-service review management providers usually run in upwards of $500 each month. Some may require you to pay annually.

2. ResellerRatings - Another expensive review site, Reseller Ratings gives you most of the benefits of the other custom-price providers. They have great SEO ranking. Your brand's Reseller Ratings

profile often appears on the first page of search results. If you already have a profile, you should maintain those reviews as well.

3. <u>Reviews.co.uk</u> - A super affordable option (as low as $89 per month), Reviews.io is a beta service provider that allows you to collect, reply and publish reviews. I see the most potential in this service provider and often recommend it to you.

4. <u>Google Reviews</u> - A free option, Google Local and Google My Business reviews for your business should always be maintained separately from any other service provider. The Google search giant may leverage these reviews in the future, and you may not know where.

5. <u>TrustPilot</u> - Another one of those expensive ones, Trustpilot gives you the same control as eKomi and Reseller Ratings. Trustpilot has good search engine ranking position so it's a good idea to maintain these stars if your profile exists. I've spent up to $1,600 each quarter to use this service.

9. Ask the Experts

Interview co-workers, colleagues, and partners. Include their quotes and expand on their insights like a journalist.

Your sources can unlock new insights and opinions for your readers. To generate new content for your site, consider insider interviews. Come up with questions to ask your friends, co-workers, and partners. These questions should yield answers that help your audience in some way. Some of these answers can be used to develop trust, share your culture, and build awareness with your readers.

If you work at a medium to large company:

Host a Q&A session with a member of your staff. Members from different departments can be fantastic resources for new material.

Here are some sample headlines I came up with to get your creative juices flowing:

10 Ways CompanyName Hits a Home Run in Customer Service
Employee of the Month Spotlight
Meet the Person Behind the Deal
The Secret Life of an Employee at Company Name

If you're self-employed or own your own business:

Ask business partners, vendors, and clients questions that help describe your benefit to prospective resources. Ask your friends and family who may be experts in their field for their perspective on a topic related to your industry.

More sample headlines:

3 Services Every CompanyName Customer Needs
Why IndustryX is not much different from IndustryY
An IndustryX Expert's Take on IndustryY

The Q&A format will be perfectly structured for a featured snippet.

Sample questions to ask:

1. How many years have you worked in the industry?

2. What's your favorite leadership quote?

3. Where/what did you study or go to school?

4. Where were you born and/or why did you choose this city for your career/life?

5. What's the #1 strategy you hope to use at CompanyName to influence growth in sales numbers and/or in team members?

6. Do you have a unique or fun hobby?

7. Have you ever shipped anything via freight? If so what was it?

8. What's the weirdest project you've ever worked on?

9. If you could work from anywhere in the world, where would that be and why?

10. Can you share any tips or secrets with your ideal customer/reader? Who is your ideal customer/reader and why?

10. Personas

Your value statements may vary by audience. Make sure you speak in a consistent voice while addressing challenges for each persona.

Your call to action or CTA should speak directly to individual readers. You should always be writing for a narrow audience. The more specific you can be, the more relevant your content is to a reader. People share relevant content they find helpful. So, how do you change your CTA depending on who's reading? Write for a narrow audience. Diversity your content by changing the intended audience. Develop personas for your buyers or readers. Do you know what fears they have? Do they enjoy sports or travel? Once you have enough traffic to sample, these demographics and audience insights can be found in Google Analytics.

What is a persona?

A persona is the essence of the person or persons who buy from you. Give your personas a name and a face so it's easy to speak to them. When changing your intended audience, you'll be writing directly to that person and you'll need to understand their wants, fears, needs, and lifestyle.

In addition to a name, your persona needs to have an age, a gender, a profession or field of study, a budget, a need for your product or service, and emotional drivers - like the fear of missing out - that motivate them to buy.

Persona Sample: Bob the Builder

Male
40-55 years old
Builder
Builds homes and buys products you sell
Worries about weather, inspectors, and going over budget

Persona Sample: Wendy the Weaver

Female
25-40 years old

Artist
Weaves baskets, wreaths and sells online
Fears that her customers won't pay high shipping costs for online orders and she has a hard time adding new products to her online store

Let's say the original blog was given the title "10 Things We Found Cheaper Online than in Store". This title is excellent because it describes exactly what the blog is about, and it works for a broad audience. By changing the target persona, you can hit the refresh button on older content that may still be highly relevant.

For Bob, narrow down your blog to include what's relevant and meaningful to him and his business. Perhaps Bob would find a blog titled "3 Big-Ticket Home Improvement Items Never to Buy in Store". On the other hand, Wendy may read your blog called "5 Ways to Save on Ecommerce Shipping". Each new blog you create will help you switch your call to actions, multiply your content, and draw new readers to your highly tailored content.

EVEN MORE CONTENT IDEAS

11. Be Your Adversary

Argue the reverse statement or opinion. Double your content by taking the opposing side on an issue.

12. Write about an Event

Is there a movie release or other newsworthy event to which your audience may relate? If so, write about it and tie it back to your industry or subject matter.

13. Expand on a Recipe or Instructions

Did you take a unique spin on a classic recipe or how-to video? Write out how to make or how to do something and share it with your audience. Use Schema markup on food and drink recipes for a chance to appear in position zero.

14. Explore History

Ever wonder what happened on that day in history? I bet your audience might too! Reflect on the past to inject new blogs with a bit of history.

15. Persuade

Expand on your bullet list of Why you're different from the competition. Do this with any list you have on your site. Link out to a page that expands on each item in the list.

SEO REPUTATION MANAGEMENT PLAYBOOK

So, your name and reputation has been dragged through the mud online? If the content is true and not libelous or false, you cannot contact the publisher to correct or unpublish the content. Your only recourse is to "push down" the bad search results by creating new, good search results. Here's my playbook for reversing online reputation damage.

Objective: To improve Search Engine Results (SERPs) that appear on the first page of Google Search for the keyword "First Name Last Name".

Key Results: Ten positive results on the first page of Google Search for the keyword "First Name Last Name".

Strategy: To optimize the keyword "First Name Last Name" by creating an online presence via directory listings, profiles, social media, and backlinks or mentions.

Challenge: News links are the most difficult to push down to the second page of SERPs as they usually have a very high Domain Authority.

Tips: Use your name when creating usernames. The more times you mention your name in a blog post or article, the better. The article(s) we're looking to replace in SERPs typically mention your first and last name a minimum of 3x and your last name 5x or more. Aim to mention your name as many times as the offending article.

Directories

Think about organizations of which you're a member and see if they offer member directories. This helps if you have a website to link back to, but it's not mandatory.

EXAMPLE: http://mediacommons.org/user/register

Publish Content

Instagram - Google monitors your Facebook and Twitter activity. Since Facebook owns Instagram, it's a good idea to set up an account. Make sure your name is in the bio. You can connect Instagram to Twitter so that it tweets a picture of your profile. This will help you grow followers and to quickly share your content.

Quora Profile - sign up for Quora and answer questions related to your profession or any topic of interest. It will help to use your name in your bios, writing in third person. If you have any interests or hobbies, blog about it here and on any free blog sites like Medium and Thrive Global.

Medium - sign up for Medium and start blogging about any topic of interest. The more content you put out on the Internet, the more your content will appear on the first page of Google.

Thrive Global - sign up for Thrive Global and start blogging about any topic of interest.

Twitter - Keep tweeting. If you create a blog on Medium or Thrive Global, promote it here. List your LinkedIn profile or blog URL in your Twitter bio.

Glassdoor - post your resume and list as public. This may or may not be an option for you.

LinkedIn - There are two ways to publish content on this channel. You can post your resume, if that's an option. Or you can write articles about any topic of interest.

YouTube - This may or may not be an option. YouTube is owned by Google so they will have a preference for this type of content. You can publish videos about topics of interest. You don't need to show your face or identify yourself other than putting your name in the video's title and description. You can even create a fresh Gmail account and sign up under a different screen name.

Change.org - Use your real name to sign petitions relating to topics of interest.

Patreon - If you have a hobby or frequently publish content, this site is for you. I don't think you need to necessarily collect a members' fee to view your content.

Relevant blogs – Reach out to someone who owns a website, pitch guest blogging or collaborating on a post with them.

Reddit - Sign up for an account and use your name as your username and post and reply often.

Ask for Mentions

LinkedIn Recommendations - ask a colleague or someone you trust for a great recommendation. These have potential to rank as a separate result in addition to your profile.

Help A Reporter Out (HARO) - check out their free account and subscribe to emails related to a topic of your choosing. You'll be sent emails twice a day with journalists asking for quotes or interviews. This will generate backlinks and mentions. Backlinks don't count unless you have your own website.

See who is writing and talking about you online

Mention.com - sign up for a free account and add your name as the keyword to monitor.

Google Alerts - sign up for free alerts that go straight to your email. Monitor your email daily for updates on recently published content that contains your first and last name.

ADDITIONAL RESOURCES

After decades of writing for websites, I've nailed down the best resources and online tools to ensure my clients use best practices that outlast dreaded algorithm updates. SEO is not a cheater's game. It is a slow process that rewards the best players. I use a combination of the following resources to earn backlinks:

Help A Reporter Out (HARO)
Buzzsumo
Mention
Google Analytics
PRUnderground
LinkedIn
Reddit
Medium
Thrive Global

At the time of writing this guide, I've gathered more than a decade experience optimizing websites for long lasting search results. Follow the following blogs and sources that are respected by my peers:

Search Engine Journal
Moz
Search Engine Roundtable
Google "Think" Blog
HubSpot

GLOSSARY OF TERMS

Authorship - have the author's name appear on the article to give it this factor for ranking.

Backlink - when a website, not your own, links to your website's content. A strong backlink profile consists of a combination of dofollow and nofollow links from pages with a high Domain Authority or Page Rank.

Domain Authority - a search engine ranking score developed by Moz. This proprietary score tells you that a website has a strong backlink profile and overall good website health.

Featured Snippet - a featured snippet is an automatic call-out box that Google may insert in the second ranked position of search results. This call-out box gives publishers the opportunity to optimize their content, usually answering frequently asked search queries.

Keywords - also known as key terms, they can be one to many words. Keywords with more than three words are usually referred to as long-tailed keywords.

Keyword Density - a percentage representing the number of times a keyword appears on a page.

Mentions - similar to backlinks, instead an external site will mention your brand name rather than linking back to your page.

Page Speed - referring to overall site health, image sizes, broken links, corrupt JavaScript or CSS files comprise your website's loading time.

Page Rank - Google's Search algorithm that determines the search engine results position ranking given to a website.

Schema - a markup language that feeds granular details about your content to search engines. Visit Schema.org for more information.

REFERENCES

1. Search Engine Optimization. Dictionary.com, URL Available: https://www.dictionary.com/browse/search-engine-optimization

2. What is SEO? Moz, URL Available: https://moz.com/learn/seo/what-is-seo

3. Voice Search. Edit, URL Available: https://edit.co.uk/blog/voice-search/#:~:text=Google%20now%20handles%20at%20least,2.4%20trillion%20searches%20in%202020.

4. Voice Search Statistics. Think with Google, URL Available: https://www.thinkwithgoogle.com/marketing-strategies/app-and-mobile/voice-search-statistics/

5. What is Latent Semantic Indexing and Why Does it Matter for Your SEO Strategy? HubSpot, URL available: https://blog.hubspot.com/marketing/what-is-latent-semantic-indexing-why-does-it-matter-for-your-seo-strategy

ABOUT THE AUTHOR

Terese Kerrigan is a digital marketing professional located in St. Petersburg, Florida. Groomed in college to be a creative writer, she's adapted what she knows about writing and applied it toward the Google algorithm. She has successfully repaired the online reputation of clients (and herself) using techniques outlined in her "SEO Reputation Management Playbook", which can be found in this book.

www.ingramcontent.com/pod-product-compliance
Lightning Source LLC
Chambersburg PA
CBHW050314220526
45465CB00005B/1982